Romance Fiction

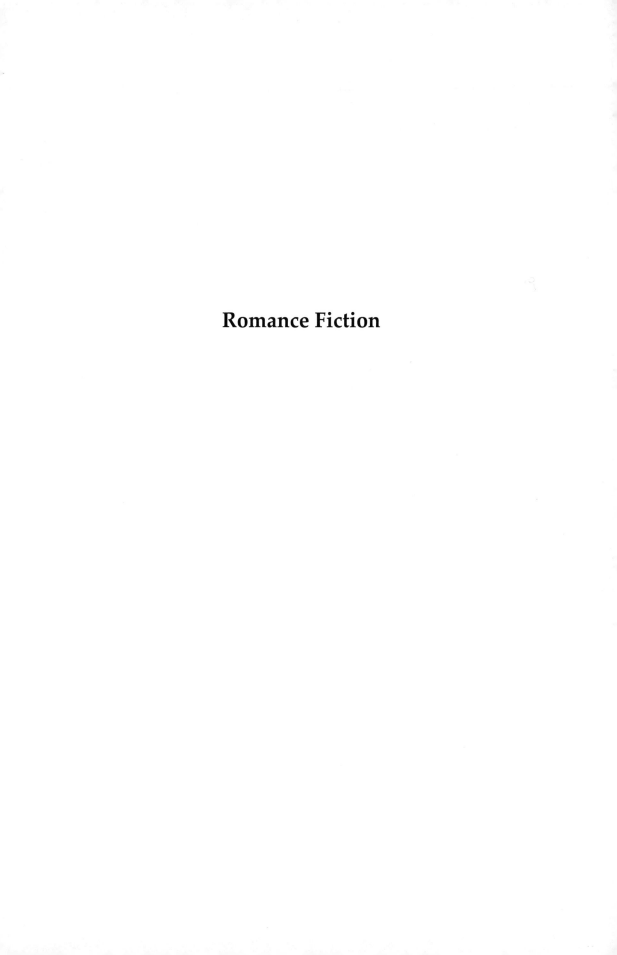

Recent Titles in
Genreflecting Advisory Series
Diana Tixier Herald, Series Editor

Latino Literature: A Guide to Reading Interests
Edited by Sara E. Martinez

Teen Chick Lit: A Guide to Reading Interests
Christine Meloni

Now Read This III: A Guide to Mainstream Fiction
Nancy Pearl and Sarah Statz Cords

Gay, Lesbian, Bisexual, Transgender and Questioning Teen Literature: A Guide to Reading Interests
Carlisle K. Webber

This is My Life: A Guide to Realistic Fiction for Teens
Rachel L. Wadham

Primary Genreflecting: A Guide to Picture Books and Easy Readers
Susan Fichtelberg and Bridget Dealy Volz

Teen Genreflecting 3: A Guide to Reading Interests
Diana Tixier Herald

Urban Grit: A Guide to Street Lit
Megan Honig

Historical Fiction for Teens: A Genre Guide
Melissa Rabey

Graphic Novels for Young Readers: A Genre Guide for Ages 4–14
Nathan Herald

Make Mine a Mystery II: A Reader's Guide to Mystery and Detective Fiction
Gary Warren Niebuhr

Mostly Manga: A Genre Guide to Popular Manga, Manwha, Manhua, an Anime
Elizabeth Kalen